W9-BNP-591

asian wraps & rolls

asian wraps & rolls

VICKI LILEY

PERIPLUS

contents

Step-by-step Wrapping & Rolling 24

Fish and Seafood 32

Duck and Chicken 52

asian wraps & rolls

ALL ABOUT
wraps & rolls

Bite-sized bundles of food are a trademark of Asian cuisine. What would the crispy spring roll or the silken wonton be without their wrappers? In China, small dumplings and rolls have been served with tea since the Sung Dynasty in the tenth century. Yet, archaeological evidence suggests that the custom of wrapping food may date back 8,000–10,000 years, when hunter-gatherers throughout the world began to form permanent settlements and cultivate cereal crops. .

By 2000BC, these crops were being cultivated on all continents, providing raw materials for the unleavened breads of the Middle East, the taco of Central America, pasta in China and Italy (think cannelloni, calzone), and the endless varieties of wrappers to be found throughout East and Southeast Asia.

Wrapper materials are not restricted to the combination of flour and water. Greek stuffed vine leaves are another example of wrapped food. Vietnamese rice paper, banana leaves, dried Japanese seaweed, lettuce leaves, betel-nut leaves, filo pastry, and even bell pepper (capsicum) shells can form the containers for an endless variety of foodstuffs.

The universal popularity of wrapped food and the ingenuity that goes into its creation has been a common theme throughout history.

Wraps and rolls represent people's energy and resourcefulness, often under difficult circumstances. There are, and always have been, areas of the world too poor for a visit to a restaurant to be anything but the greatest luxury. Cutlery is a relatively recent invention. Instead, millions of people are used to gathering to share food, eaten with their bare hands, in crowded alleys, under trees, around a cooking fire or grabbing a quick bite from a street vendor. This is honest food, durable and adaptable food. It's survival cuisine, food for all classes and ages—real food.

Today, wrapped food is as relevant as ever. Its diversity and versatility make it is ideal for any meal, from appetizers to mains. It also makes great hors d'oeuvres and finger food for entertaining.

Given the enormous range of wraps and rolls available, this book does not restrict the reader to Asia, a broad enough canvas in itself. The aim has been to recreate the fun and excitement of traditional Asian street food, the kinds of food you're drawn to automatically as you walk down any street in the tropics and catch the aromas of fresh ingredients steaming, frying, bubbling in a pot, or sizzling in a wok or kadai.

For those with a passion for Asian spices, spice blends, contrasting textures, colors, smells and cooking techniques, you will be satisfied, too. Add to that the Western convenience of unleavened breads, dinner rolls as wraps, and ready-made puff and filo pastries and you have a great way of saving time, money and kitchen slavery. Perhaps the greatest bonus of embracing wraps and rolls is that you'll have a convenient means of introducing spicy Asian flavors and unusual ingredients to your family—even the kids.

Be brave and experiment with different foods and food combinations. Use this book as a starting point for your own culinary inventions. Involve the entire family in preparing the meal by arranging the ingredients in serving dishes and letting everyone assemble their own. Extend the snack concept to provide an assortment of temptations as a main meal for family and friends. Accompany your offerings with a range of tasty dipping sauces, and sit back and reap the satisfaction of having topped the hospitality stakes.

BANANA LEAVES

Banana leaves

Sections of the large, glossy green leaves of the banana tree are used to wrap foods for steaming, boiling, and grilling. The leaves keep the food inside moist and add a distinctive flavor to savory and sweet dishes. Available at Asian markets. Store in a plastic bag in the refrigerator for up to 7 days.

BETEL LEAVES

Betel leaves

The thick, smooth edible green leaves of the betel pepper (pan plant) are broad at one end and pointed at the other. Used to wrap Asian foods. Available from Asian markets, or order in advance from specialty produce markets. Use lettuce leaves or large basil leaves as a substitute.

Lettuce leaves

Butter, iceberg, and radicchio leaves make easy, instant wraps for hot and cold spicy fillings. Lettuce leaves can also add texture and flavor when used with fresh rice paper wrappers.

LETTUCE LEAVES

Nori, dried

Nori seaweed is packaged in various different forms and shapes. The most common is used for making sushi or rolled sushi. These delicate sheets are available toasted or untoasted, and are typically sold in a package of 10-by-7-by-8-inch (25-by-18-by-20-cm) sheets. Once opened, they should be kept in airtight bags, in a cool, dark place. Other varieties include a seasoned version, which is generally shredded and used to garnish steamed rice. When rolling with nori, make sure the smooth, glossy side is facing out.

NORI DRIED

Dinner rolls

Small dinner rolls or bagels make ideal party-sized containers for grilled meats.

DINNER ROLLS

Flour tortillas

Round unleavened Mexican breads, sold in packets in supermarkets.

FLOUR TORTILLAS

Lavash

A rectangular, unleavened bread, sold in packets. Ideal for wrapping foods.

LAVASH

MOUNTAIN BREAD

Mountain bread

A square, thin, unleavened Middle Eastern bread, sold in packets. Ideal for wrapping foods.

Naan

Oval-shaped unleavened Indian bread, available at some supermarkets. To heat, follow directions on packet.

NAAN

SLICED BREAD

Sliced bread

White, whole-wheat (wholemeal) or multigrain bread can be used to wrap foods. Trim crusts before using.

Filo dough

Also spelled phyllo. A paper-thin dough made from flour and water, available frozen in supermarkets. Thaw in the refrigerator. Keep this dough covered with a damp cloth while working with it, as it dries out quickly.

Puff pastry

Available in ready-made rolled sheets in the freezer section of most supermarkets.

Rice paper wrappers

Originating in Vietnam, these fragile round or square wrappers are made from rice flour and water. Traditionally, batter was poured onto woven mats and then left to dry in the sun. The wrappers are used, uncooked, to wrap food. They may also be deep-fried. They are available fresh or dried at Asian markets. Soak in warm water for 15–30 seconds before use.

FILO DOUGH

PUFF PASTRY

RICE PAPER WRAPPERS

Spring roll wrappers

A very thin crepe made from flour and water. Spring roll wrappers are sold frozen in packages of around 10 or 25, either $8\frac{1}{2}$ inches (21.5 cm) square or round. Available in Asian markets and many supermarkets. Thaw in the refrigerator before opening the package. Trim the edges of the wrappers for easier separation. Seal and store unused wrappers in the refrigerator for up to 7 days, or refreeze for up to 1 month.

SPRING ROLL WRAPPERS

Wonton skins and potsticker wrappers

Yellow wonton skins are made from an egg-based dough, while white dumpling wrappers, also called potsticker wrappers or "gow gee", are made from a wheat-based dough. Generally, the wrappers are used for steamed or boiled dumplings. Wonton skins are used for boiled or fried wontons. They are usually $3\frac{1}{2}$ inches (9 cm) square, though they also may be round.

Widely available fresh or frozen in Asian markets. Fresh wrappers will keep for up to 7 days in the refrigerator. Wrappers may be frozen.

WONTON SKINS

Basil: A sweet-tasting herb with a slightly licorice flavor. Leaves are used whole or chopped.

Thai basil: Also known as holy basil, this herb has a strong, distinctive flavor.

Cilantro (coriander): An essential herb in Asian cooking. Also known as Chinese parsley. Leaves, stems, and roots may be used. Do not chop the leaves too finely, as they will darken and lose their flavor.

Vietnamese mint: A spicy hot variety of mint that is delicious in salads. Substitute with basic mint if unavailable.

Bok choy sum: Also known as flowering bok chow, flowering cabbage, or choy sum. Probably the most well-known and available Chinese green. It has yellow flowers, thin stems, and a mild flavor. It is suitable in most recipes that call for Chinese greens. The entire vegetable (stem, leaves, and flowers) is used.

Chinese lettuce: A curly variety of lettuce, available at Asian stores. Use butter or romaine (cos) lettuce if unavailable.

Fresh bean sprouts: Sprouting green mung beans. Store in the refrigerator for 2–3 days.

Shimeji mushrooms: Also known as oyster mushrooms. Straw-colored cultivated mushrooms that grow in short clumps and have small caps.

Warning about chilies: Take special care not to touch your face or eyes when handling chilies, and always wash your hands thoroughly after touching raw chilies, or wear disposable gloves. Using a sharp knife, cut the chili in half lengthwise. Scrape seeds from chili (or you may leave in the seeds for a hotter flavor). Remove the white pith (membrane) from the chili. The seeds contain some heat, but the real source of heat is the capsaicin found in the white pith.

Bird's eye red chilies: A small, blazing hot chili, with a clear fiery taste. Use in small quantities.

Thai chilies: These medium-hot red or green chilies grow to 1½ inches (4 cm) long. They are available in most produce markets. Also called Thai dragon chilies. The somewhat milder green or red Anaheim chili pepper, similarly shaped and up to 6 inches (15 cm) long, may be substituted.

Chinese sausages: Sweet, dry, and spicy pork sausages (lop chong) are sold in airtight unrefrigerated packets or in the refrigerator section of Asian markets, or they may be found hanging from string in Chinese delis. Red in color. Dark brown duck liver sausages are also sold. Steam before eating plain or stir-frying.

Cellophane noodles: Thin, translucent dried noodles, also called bean thread noodles. Cellophane noodles are delicious deep-fried and used in fillings for a crisp texture or as a crunchy nest for stir-fries. Or, soften them in hot water and use in soups, stir-fries, and fillings. Use rice stick vermicelli or angel hair pasta if unavailable.

Fried noodles (flour sticks): Crispy fried noodles, sold in packages. Use as garnish or serve with stir-fries. Available in Asian markets. If unavailable, simply deep-fry fresh egg noodles in hot oil until crisp.

Fried shallots (French shallots): Commonly used as a garnish for Asian dishes. Thin slices of small red shallots are cut lengthwise and deep-fried until golden and crisp. Available dried in packages at Asian markets. Store in an airtight container in the freezer to prevent them from going rancid.

Fried tofu skins (abura-age): A Japanese ingredient, used as pouches for fillings. Available at Asian or Japanese markets.

Chinese barbecued pork: Also known as char siew. A fatty, boneless piece of pork, marinated and roasted. Sold sliced or whole in Chinese delis. Requires no further cooking. Store in the refrigerator for up to 2 days.

Chinese roast duck: Sold in Chinese delis, usually seen hanging in the window. May be purchased whole or by the half, chopped or not. Delicious on its on or use in fillings or salads. Store in the refrigerator for up to 2 days. Use roast chicken if unavailable.

Chinese roast pork: Roasted pork belly with a crisp crackling crust. Usually seen hanging in the window of Chinese delis. Sold by weight, chopped or whole. Substitute Chinese barbecued pork or roast pork slices from a regular deli.

Chinese soy chicken: A glossy, golden chicken, glazed in soy, usually seen hanging in the window of Chinese delis. Delicious on its own or used in fillings or salads. Generally sold with a ginger dipping sauce. Store in the refrigerator for up to 2 days. Roast chicken may be substituted.

Chili oil

An extremely hot oil, used in small quantities. Made from frying chilies in either sesame or vegetable oil.

Hoisin sauce

Also known as Chinese barbecue sauce, it is made from soybeans, sugar, vinegar, salt, garlic, and chilies. Store in the refrigerator after opening.

Fish sauce

Known as nam pla in Thailand, and nuoc mam in Vietnam. It has a strong fishy smell and a salty taste. Used in sauces, dressings, and dipping sauces. There is no substitute. Store in the refrigerator after opening.

Ketjap manis

A sweetened Indonesian soy sauce that is much thicker and darker in appearance than regular soy. Use as a dipping sauce or for marinating.

Mirin

A gold-colored sweet Japanese rice wine made from sake in varying strengths. Use in salads, marinades, and stir-fries.

Sambal oelek

A spicy Indonesian paste consisting of ground chili peppers, salt, and occasionally vinegar. It can be used as a substitute for fresh chili peppers. Store in the refrigerator after opening.

Shaoxing wine

Also known as rice wine, made from glutinous rice. Substitute dry sherry.

Soy sauce

Available in light and dark varieties. Dark soy is usually used in cooking, and the lighter soy for dipping sauces.

Tamarind paste

Sold in jars and tubes in Asian markets. Made from the acid-tasting fruit of a large tropical tree. If unavailable, substitute fresh lime juice. Store in the refrigerator after opening.

Thai sweet chili sauce

A mild chili sauce with a sweet aftertaste. Usually used as a dipping sauce, it can also be used on burgers and grilled meats. Store in the refrigerator after opening.

COOKING
equipment

The wok is a great addition to the kitchen, as it is especially suitable for steaming, stir-frying, and deep-frying.

Carbon-steel or rolled-steel woks, the popular, inexpensive woks found in Asian stores, are coated with a thin film of lacquer to keep them from rusting. This film needs to be removed before the wok can be used.

To remove film of lacquer from wok: Place the wok on the stovetop. Fill with cold water, and add 2 tablespoons of baking soda (bicarbonate of soda). Bring to a boil and boil rapidly for 15 minutes. Drain, scrub off the varnish with a plastic scourer, and repeat the process if any lacquer remains. Then rinse and dry the wok. It is now ready to be seasoned.

Carbon-steel, rolled-steel and cast-iron woks require seasoning before use in order to keep food from sticking to the wok and to prevent the wok from discoloring.

To season a wok: Place the wok over low heat. Have a roll of paper towels and a container of vegetable oil handy. When the wok is hot, carefully wipe it with a piece of oiled paper towel. Repeat the process with fresh paper until it comes away clean and without any trace of color on it.

A seasoned wok should not be cleaned with soap, as this will remove the seasoning. To clean, use hot water and a sponge or plastic scrubber. Dry the wok well after washing. Store your wok in a dry, well-ventilated place. Long periods without use can cause the oil coating on the wok to become rancid. Using your wok frequently is the best way to keep this from happening.

A number of cooking utensils go hand in hand with a wok, including the bamboo steamer. Available at Asian supermarkets in a variety of sizes, these can be stacked on top of each other in a wok of simmering water, allowing the cook to prepare an entire meal at one time while using minimal electricity or gas. Bamboo steamers need only be rinsed in hot water after cooking.

A Chinese wire-mesh skimmer with a bamboo handle is perfect for removing deep-fried foods from hot oil. Long, cooking chopsticks and wooden tongs are also handy utensils for cooking Asian dishes.

A sushi mat is helpful in preparing sushi. Parchment (baking) paper is an attractive way to secure and serve bread wraps and rolls.

wrapping & rolling

Shrimp and cilantro rolls

(see page 34 for recipe)

1   Remove crusts from bread slices.

2   Roll bread flat, using a rolling pin.

3   Spread about 1 tablespoonful of prawn filling over each slice of bread.

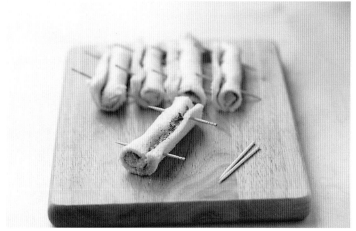

4   Roll up each and secure with 2 toothpicks.

Preparing tuna spring rolls

(see page 40 for recipe)

1   Using a sharp knife, cut tuna into slices ¾ inch (2 cm) wide by 3 inches (7.5 cm) long.

2   Lightly spread each piece of tuna with wasabi paste.

3   Wrap each piece of tuna in a betel leaf (trim leaf to size if necessary).

4   Place a spring roll wrapper on a work surface with one end facing you. Brush wrapper with egg white. Place a tuna parcel 1 inch (2.5 cm) from end of wrapper. Roll bottom of wrapper over, fold in sides and roll up. Cover with plastic.

Fish in banana leaves

(see page 48 for recipe)

1   Place a piece of fish in the center of each leaf.

2   Divide herb mixture among fish pieces. Spread over top of fish.

3   Fold sides of banana leaves over like a package and secure with a short bamboo skewer.

4   Place fish parcels in a baking dish. Bake for 15 minutes.

Bite-sized oyster rolls

(see page 50 for recipe)

1 Place a wonton skin on a work surface with one end facing you (keep remaining skins covered with a damp cloth to prevent drying out).

2 Place 1 oyster ½ inch (12 mm) from end of skin. Spoon about ½ teaspoonful of ginger mixture on top of oyster.

3 Brush edges of skin with water.

4 Fold the bottom of skin over oyster. Fold in sides and roll up. Cover with a damp cloth. Repeat with remaining skins, oysters, and ginger mixture.

Tiny pork rolls

(see page 68 for recipe)

1 Using scissors, cut rice paper wrappers into quarters.

2 Working in batches, brush each wrapper with beaten egg. Allow to stand 2–3 minutes, or until softened.

3 Place 1 heaped teaspoonful of pork filling near the rounded end of each quarter.

4 Fold the rounded end of wrapper over filling. Fold in sides and roll into a small cylinder.

Pork and shrimp rolls

(see page 72 for recipe)

1 Fill a medium bowl with warm water and place a clean kitchen towel on your work surface. Dip 2 rice paper wrappers in the water for 15 seconds, or until soft. Stack wrappers on the kitchen towel.

2 Place a lettuce leaf on one side of stacked papers. Top with 1 tablespoonful of mayonnaise. Arrange $\frac{1}{8}$ of noodles and pork over lettuce leaf. Top with 3 mint leaves.

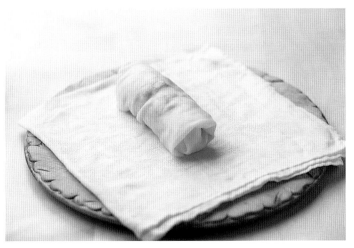

3 Starting at lettuce side of wrapper, roll halfway into a cylinder. Lay 2 shrimp halves, cut-side down, on wrapper.

4 Continue to roll into a cylinder. Cover roll with a damp kitchen towel to prevent drying out. Repeat with remaining wrappers and filling.

Asian sausage rolls

(see page 78 for recipe)

1   Using a sharp knife, trim sausage ends.

2   Working in batches, cut each pastry sheet into four equal squares. Brush edges with beaten egg.

3   Turn squares so that one corner faces you. Place a sausage diagonally across each pastry square, placing it slightly towards the bottom of the square.

4   Fold pastry over sausage, tucking in sides, and roll to form a cylinder. Brush top with beaten egg. Sprinkle with sesame seeds. Bake for 15 minutes.

Tofu and rice wraps

(see page 92 for recipe)

1 In a saucepan of boiling water, cook the tofu skins for 3 minutes. Using a slotted spoon, transfer to paper towels to drain. Cut each tofu skin in half. Open each half to make a pouch.

2 Using wet hands, place about ¼ cup of the sushi rice mixture into a tofu pouch. Do not overfill, or the pouch will split. Put the filled pouches, open-side up, on a cutting board or plate.

3 Tie a scallion length around each tofu pouch. Refrigerate for 1–2 hours before serving.

Crispy wrapped shrimp

FOR FILLING

4 oz (125 g) ground (minced) pork

2 cloves garlic, finely chopped

1 teaspoon peeled and grated fresh ginger

1 tablespoon chopped fresh cilantro
(fresh coriander)

1 scallion (shallot/spring onion), finely chopped

1 teaspoon soy sauce

12 jumbo shrimp (king prawns), shelled
(tails intact)

12 frozen square spring roll wrappers
(8$^1/_2$ by 8$^1/_2$ inches/21.5 by 21.5 cm), thawed

1 egg white, lightly beaten

3 cups (24 fl oz/750 ml) vegetable or canola oil
for deep-frying

2 lime wedges for serving

$^1/_3$ cup (3 fl oz/80 ml) Thai sweet chili sauce
for dipping

To make filling: In a bowl, combine pork, garlic, ginger, cilantro, scallion, and soy sauce. Mix until well combined. Set aside. Cut halfway through the back of each shrimp. Remove the dark vein from each and open shrimp flat. Spread about 1–2 teaspoons of pork mixture on one side of each shrimp. Press shrimp sides back together.

Place 1 spring roll wrapper on a work surface. Fold wrapper in half diagonally. Brush wrapper surface with egg white. Place a shrimp on wrapper 1 inch (2.5 cm) from end, allowing its tail to overhang edge of wrapper. Roll bottom of wrapper over shrimp, leaving shrimp tail unwrapped. Fold in sides and roll up. Again, leave shrimp tail unwrapped. Cover with plastic wrap and repeat with remaining ingredients.

In a wok, a large, heavy-based skillet, or a deep fryer, heat oil to 375°F (190°C), or until a small cube of bread dropped in the oil sizzles and turns golden. Working with 2 shrimp wraps at a time, deep-fry until golden and crisp, 3–4 minutes. Using a wire-mesh skimmer, transfer to paper towels to drain. Serve hot, with lime wedges, and Thai sweet chili sauce as a dipping sauce.

Makes 12 wraps

Shrimp and cilantro rolls

(see page 24 for step-by-step guide)

FOR FILLING

8 oz (250 g) jumbo shrimp (king prawns), peeled
and deveined

2 scallions (shallots/spring onions),
finely chopped

2 cloves garlic, finely chopped

1 bird's eye red chili, seeded and chopped

2 tablespoons chopped fresh cilantro
(fresh coriander)

12 slices white sandwich bread, crusts trimmed

3 cups (24 fl oz/750 ml) vegetable or canola oil
for deep-frying

1/3 cup (3 fl oz/80 ml) Thai sweet chili sauce for
dipping

To make filling: In a food processor, process shrimp until smooth. Transfer to a bowl. Stir in scallions, garlic, chili, and cilantro. Mix until well combined. Using a rolling pin, press bread slices flat. Spread about 1 tablespoonful of shrimp filling over each slice of bread. Roll up and secure with 2 toothpicks.

In a large, heavy skillet, or a deep fryer, heat oil until it reaches 375°F (190°C) or until a small bread cube dropped in oil sizzles and turns golden. Working in batches, add shrimp rolls and fry until golden, 1–2 minutes. Using a wire-mesh skimmer, transfer to paper towels to drain. Serve hot, with chili sauce.

Makes 12 rolls

Warm mango and shrimp wraps

2 tablespoons vegetable oil

2 cloves garlic, finely chopped

1 Thai red chili, seeded and sliced

16 oz (500 g) jumbo shrimp (king prawns), peeled
  and deveined (tails intact)

juice of 1 lime

$^1/_4$ cup (2 fl oz/60 ml) Thai sweet chili sauce

4 pieces mountain bread or lavash, halved

1 ripe mango, peeled, cut from pit, and sliced

24 fresh basil leaves

12 fresh mint leaves

Heat oil in a wok or large, heavy skillet over medium heat and stir-fry garlic and chili for 1 minute, or until fragrant. Add shrimp and stir-fry until pink, 3–4 minutes. Remove wok from heat. Stir in lime juice and chili sauce. Let cool for 5 minutes.

Place bread on a work surface. Arrange shrimp mixture, mango, basil, and mint evenly over bread. Roll up each and wrap with a piece of parchment (baking) paper. Serve immediately.

Makes 8 wraps

WARM MANGO AND SHRIMP WRAPS

Salmon sushi rolls

4 oz (125 g) sashimi-grade salmon fillet, pin bones and
  skin removed

2 sheets toasted nori

vinegared rice (see below)

about $^1/_4$–$^1/_2$ teaspoon wasabi paste

$^1/_3$ cup (3 fl oz/80 ml) light soy sauce

VINEGARED RICE

FOR RICE

$1^1/_4$ cups (9 oz/280 g) short-grain rice

$1^1/_4$ cups (10 fl oz/300 ml) water

$1^1/_2$ tablespoons sake

FOR VINEGAR

$1^1/_2$ tablespoons sushi vinegar

$^1/_4$ teaspoon sea salt

1 teaspoon superfine (caster) sugar

Cut salmon into $^3/_8$-inch (1-cm) square sticks. Place a sushi mat on a work surface. Cut each nori sheet in half. Place 1 piece nori on the sushi mat.

With wet hands, put 2–3 tablespoonfuls of vinegared rice in one hand. Make a log shape with the rice, and place it in the center of the nori. Using your hands, spread rice evenly over nori, leaving a $^1/_2$-inch (12-mm) border. Take a small dot of wasabi paste and draw a line down the center of the rice. Arrange a stick of salmon over the wasabi. Pick up sushi mat from side nearest you. Roll mat over to meet other side, making sure rice stays inside the nori. Lift top edge of mat and press and roll cylinder slightly, seam-side down. Transfer to a cutting board. Repeat with remaining nori and filling. To serve, cut each roll into 6 pieces. Serve with soy sauce for dipping.

Makes about 24 pieces

Vinegared rice: Put rice into a bowl, and add cold water to cover. Stir briskly to remove any starch. Drain. Repeat 3 times.

Pour rice and $1^1/_4$ cups water in a medium, heavy saucepan. Cover and bring to a boil. Boil for 3 minutes. Reduce heat to medium and boil for 5 minutes. Reduce heat to low and simmer for 5–10 minutes, or until rice is tender. Remove from heat and stir in sake. Place a kitchen towel over open pan. Replace lid and let rice stand for 15 minutes. Scrape hot rice into a shallow dish and spread out evenly. Stir rice to separate grains. Gradually stir in vinegar and continue stirring until rice is at room temperature. (Do not refrigerate.) Cover with a damp kitchen towel.

To make vinegar: In a small saucepan, combine vinegar, salt, and sugar. Stir over low heat until sugar dissolves. Remove from heat.

SALMON SUSHI ROLLS

Crisp-fried tuna spring rolls

(see page 25 for step-by-step guide)

8 oz (500 g) piece sashimi-quality tuna

1–2 teaspoons wasabi paste, to taste

8 fresh betel leaves or large basil leaves

8 frozen square (8$^1/_2$ by 8$^1/_2$ inches/21.5 by
  21.5 cm) spring roll wrappers, thawed

1 egg white, lightly beaten

3 cups (24 fl oz/750 ml) vegetable or canola oil
  for deep-frying

3 tablespoons light soy sauce

Using a sharp knife, cut tuna into slices ¾ inch (2 cm) wide and 3 inches (7.5 cm) long. Lightly spread each piece of tuna with wasabi paste.

Wrap each piece of tuna in a betel leaf (trim leaf to size if necessary). Place a spring roll wrapper on a work surface with one end facing you. Brush wrapper with egg white. Place a tuna parcel 1 inch (2.5 cm) from end of wrapper and roll end of wrapper over. Fold in sides and roll up. Cover with plastic wrap. Repeat with remaining wrappers and filling.

In a wok, a large, heavy skillet, or a deep fryer, heat oil to 375°F (190°C) or until a small bread cube dropped in oil sizzles and turns golden. Working in batches, add tuna rolls and fry until golden, 1–2 minutes. Using a wire-mesh skimmer, transfer to paper towels to drain. Serve immediately, whole or sliced, with soy sauce for dipping.

Makes 8 rolls

Hints

For best results, tuna is served pink on the inside.

CRISP-FRIED TUNA SPRING ROLLS

Spicy crab in lettuce bowls

2 tablespoons vegetable or canola oil

2 cloves garlic, finely chopped

2 teaspoons peeled and grated fresh ginger

1 bird's eye red chili, seeded and chopped

4 scallions (shallots/spring onions), sliced

8 oz (500 g) fresh lump crabmeat, picked over
for shell

1 fresh kaffir lime leaf, finely shredded

2 tablespoons chopped fresh cilantro
(fresh coriander)

1 tablespoon finely chopped fresh mint

grated zest and juice of 1 lime

1 teaspoon fish sauce

4 iceberg lettuce leaves

Heat oil in a wok or medium skillet over medium heat and stir-fry garlic, ginger, and chili for 1 minute, or until aromatic. Add scallions, crabmeat, and lime leaf. Stir-fry for 3 minutes.

Remove from heat and stir in cilantro, mint, lime zest and juice, and fish sauce. Let stand for 5 minutes. Put each lettuce leaf in a serving bowl, spoon in warm filling, and serve immediately.

Makes 4 bowls

Shrimp and papaya fresh spring rolls

1 small papaya, peeled and seeded

16 round rice paper wrappers
  (8¹/₂ inches/21.5 cm in diameter)

32 jumbo shrimp (king prawns), cooked, shelled,
  and deveined

¹/₂ cup (4 fl oz/125 ml) Thai sweet chili sauce

32 fresh cilantro (fresh coriander) leaves

32 fresh mint leaves

¹/₂ cup (4 fl oz/125 ml) Thai sweet chili sauce
  for dipping

Cut papaya into 16 wedges. Fill a bowl with warm water and place a clean kitchen towel on your work surface. Dip a rice paper wrapper into the water for 15 seconds or until soft, then place on kitchen towel. Arrange 1 slice papaya, 2 shrimp, 2 teaspoonfuls chili sauce, 2 cilantro leaves and 2 mint leaves on one side of wrapper. Roll into a cylinder. Transfer to a plate and cover with a damp towel to prevent drying out. Repeat with remaining wrappers and filling.

Serve with Thai sweet chili sauce for dipping.

Makes 16 rolls

SHRIMP AND PAPAYA FRESH SPRING ROLLS

Breaded seafood wraps

8 boneless, skinless white fish fillets
(about 5 oz/150 g each)

16 jumbo shrimp (king prawns), shelled and
deveined (tails intact)

1 tablespoon vegetable oil

1 tablespoon fresh lime juice

2 cloves garlic, finely chopped

1 egg, beaten with 3 tablespoons milk

$^1/_2$ cup dried bread crumbs

3 cups (24 fl oz/750 ml) vegetable or canola oil
for deep-frying

$^1/_2$ cup (4 fl oz/125 ml) Thai sweet chili sauce

Cut each fish fillet in half horizontally. Wrap 1 piece fish around each shrimp and secure with a toothpick. In a small bowl, stir oil, lime juice, and garlic together. Brush wrapped rolls with oil mixture, then cover with plastic wrap and refrigerate for 30 minutes.

Dip wrapped rolls in egg mixture, then roll in bread crumbs to coat. In a large, heavy skillet, deep fryer, or wok, heat oil to 375°F (190°C), or until a small bread cube dropped in oil sizzles and turns golden. Working in batches, fry fish and shrimp wraps until golden, 2–3 minutes. Using a wire-mesh skimmer, transfer to paper towels to drain. Serve hot, with chili sauce for dipping.

Makes 16 wraps

BREADED SEAFOOD WRAPS

Fish wrapped in banana leaves

(see page 26 for step-by-step guide)

$^{1}/_{3}$ cup ($^{1}/_{2}$ oz/15 g) chopped fresh cilantro
  (fresh coriander)

2 tablespoons finely chopped Vietnamese mint

3 cloves garlic, finely chopped

1 Thai red chili, seeded and finely chopped

1 tablespoon grated lime zest

3 teaspoons peeled and grated fresh ginger

2 tablespoons fresh lime juice

4 pieces fresh banana leaf or parchment (baking)
  paper, each 8 inches (20 cm) square

4 salmon or ocean trout fillets, skin and pin
  bones removed

steamed white rice for serving (optional)

Preheat oven to 400°F (200°C). In a medium bowl, combine cilantro, mint, garlic, chili, lime zest, ginger, and juice. Stir until well combined.

Place banana leaf squares on a work surface. Place a piece of fish in the center of each leaf. Divide herb mixture among fish pieces and spread over top of fish. Fold sides of banana leaf square over like a package and secure with a short bamboo skewer. Place fish parcels in a baking dish.

Bake for 15 minutes. Remove from oven and place on serving plates. Open parcels at table. Serve with steamed rice.

Makes 4 parcels

FISH WRAPPED IN BANANA LEAVES

Bite-sized oyster rolls

(see page 27 for step-by-step guide)

2 tablespoons peeled and grated fresh ginger

1 tablespoon chopped fresh cilantro
  (fresh coriander)

1 tablespoon finely chopped scallion
  (shallot/spring onion)

1 teaspoon grated lime zest

1 teaspoon fresh lime juice

1 teaspoon Asian sesame oil

24 square wonton skins

24 fresh oysters

3 cups (24 fl oz/750 ml) vegetable or canola oil
  for deep-frying

Lime and soy dipping sauce (see page 106)

In a small bowl, combine ginger, cilantro, scallion, lime zest and juice, and sesame oil. Stir until well combined.

Place 1 wonton skin on work surface with corner facing towards you (keep remaining skins covered with a damp cloth to prevent drying out). Place 1 oyster diagonally across bottom corner of skin. Spoon about $\frac{1}{2}$ teaspoonful of ginger mixture on top of oyster. Brush edges with water. Fold bottom corner of skin over oyster. Fold in sides and roll. Cover with a damp cloth and repeat with remaining skins and filling.

In a wok, a large heavy skillet, or a deep fryer, heat vegetable oil to 375°F (190°C) or until a small bread cube dropped in oil sizzles and turns golden. Working in batches, fry oyster rolls until golden, about 2 minutes. Using a wire-mesh skimmer, transfer to paper towels to drain. Serve hot, with dipping sauce.

Makes 24 rolls

BITE-SIZED OYSTER ROLLS

chicken

Chinese ham and chicken rolls

$^1/_2$ teaspoon salt

$^1/_4$ teaspoon ground white pepper

$^1/_4$ teaspoon Chinese five-spice powder

1 clove garlic, finely chopped

4 boneless, skinless chicken breast fillets

4 thin slices ham

4 frozen square spring roll wrappers (8$^1/_2$ by
   8$^1/_2$ inches/21.5 by 21.5 cm), thawed

$^1/_4$ cup (1$^1/_2$ oz/45 g) all-purpose (plain) flour

1 egg, beaten with 2 tablespoons milk

3 cups (24 fl oz/750 ml) vegetable or canola oil
   for deep-frying

$^1/_2$ cup (4 fl oz/125 ml) Thai sweet chili sauce

In a small bowl, combine salt, pepper, five-spice powder, and garlic. Stir to blend.

Place a chicken breast in between 2 sheets of plastic wrap. Using a meat mallet, pound very thin. Spread chicken with garlic mixture. Roll a slice of ham and place at one end of chicken. Fold sides of chicken in, then roll chicken around ham to form a log. Repeat with remaining chicken, garlic mixture and ham.

Place 1 spring roll wrapper on a work surface, with a corner facing you. Coat 1 chicken log in flour, then in egg mixture. Place chicken diagonally across wrapper, 1 inch (2.5 cm) from bottom. Fold in sides and roll up securely. Bunch edge of wrapper with egg mixture and seal.

In a large, heavy skillet, deep fryer, or wok, heat oil to 375°F (190°C) or until a small bread cube dropped in oil sizzles and turns golden. Working in batches, fry ham and chicken rolls until golden, 3–4 minutes. Using a wire-mesh skimmer, transfer to paper towels to drain.

Let stand for 3 minutes before slicing. Serve hot, with chili sauce for dipping.

Makes 4 rolls

CHINESE HAM AND CHICKEN ROLLS

Soy chicken and noodle rolls

1 oz (30 g) cellophane noodles

1 tablespoon dried shrimp, finely chopped or
  ground in a mortar and pestle

8 cherry tomatoes, quartered

$^{1}/_{2}$ red onion, thinly sliced

1–2 red bird's eye chilies, seeded and chopped
  to taste

2 tablespoons shredded fresh basil

2 tablespoons roasted peanuts

8 oz (250 g) boneless Chinese soy chicken and skin

8 round rice paper wrappers (8 inches /20 cm in
  diameter)

4 butter lettuce leaves

1 tablespoon fried shallots (French shallots)

Ginger and lime dipping sauce (page 102)

FOR THE DRESSING

1 tablespoon fresh lime juice

1 tablespoon fish sauce

1 teaspoon tamarind paste

2 teaspoons superfine (caster) sugar

Put noodles in a bowl, and add boiling water to cover. Let soak for 10 minutes. Drain. Using scissors, coarsely cut noodles into shorter lengths. In a bowl, combine shrimp, tomatoes, onion, chili, basil, peanuts, and noodles. Stir until well combined.

Cut chicken meat and skin into thin strips about 2½ inches (6 cm) long. Combine all dressing ingredients in a screwtop jar and shake to mix. Add chicken and dressing to noodle mixture. Toss to combine. Cover and refrigerate for at least 30 minutes or up to 1 hour.

Remove about 2 inches (5 cm) of center stem from each lettuce leaf. Fill a medium bowl with warm water and place a kitchen towel on your work surface. For each roll, dip 2 rice paper wrappers into water for 15 seconds, or until soft. Stack wrappers on kitchen towel. Arrange a lettuce leaf on one side of rice paper. Spoon over one-fourth of chicken mixture. Sprinkle with fried shallots and spread mixture over lettuce leaf. Starting at lettuce side of wrapper, roll into a cylinder. Cover prepared rolls with a damp kitchen towel to prevent drying out. Repeat with remaining wrappers and filling.

Using a sharp knife, cut each roll into 2 or 3 slices. Serve with Ginger and lime dipping sauce (see page 102).

Makes 4 rolls

Hint

Substitute roast chicken if Chinese soy chicken is

unavailable.

SOY CHICKEN AND NOODLE ROLLS

Baked chicken purses

1 tablespoon vegetable oil

4 cloves garlic, finely chopped

1 bird's eye chili, seeded and finely chopped

6 1/2 oz (200 g) ground (minced) chicken

3 tablespoons Thai sweet chili sauce

2 teaspoons fish sauce

1 tablespoon chopped fresh Thai basil

2 tablespoons chopped fresh cilantro
   (fresh coriander)

sea salt and freshly ground pepper to taste

5 scallions (shallots/spring onions)

5 sheets frozen ready-made puff pastry sheets,
   thawed

1 egg, beaten

Lemon and chili dipping sauce (see page 104)
   or soy sauce for dipping

Heat oil in a wok over medium heat and stir-fry garlic and chili for 1 minute, or until fragrant. Add chicken and stir-fry until opaque, about 3 minutes. Remove from heat. Stir in chili sauce, fish sauce, basil, cilantro, salt and pepper. Mix well. Let cool completely.

Meanwhile, cut each scallion into 4 pieces lengthwise. Put in a bowl and add boiling water to cover. Let stand for 1 minute. Drain and rinse under cold running water. Drain again.

Preheat oven to 425°F (220°C). Line 2 baking trays with parchment (baking) paper. Using a 1/4-inch (6-mm) cutter, cut puff pastry into 20 rounds. Spoon 2–3 teaspoonfuls of chicken filling into center of each round. Brush edges of each round with egg. Fold pastry over filling to form a semicircle, and press edges firmly together. Tie a scallion length around each. Place on prepared paper. Brush with beaten egg.

Bake until golden and crisp, 12–15 minutes. Serve warm, with dipping sauce or soy sauce.

Makes 20 purses

BAKED CHICKEN PURSES

Warm tandoori chicken wraps

¹/₃ cup (3 fl oz/80 ml) plain tandoori paste

2 tablespoons plus ½ cup (4 oz/125 g)
　plain yogurt

grated zest and juice of 1 lemon

12 chicken tenderloin fillets or 3 skinless, boneless
　chicken breast fillets

2 carrots, peeled

1 English (hothouse) cucumber, halved and seeded

6 pieces naan

1 clove garlic, finely chopped

leaves from 6 fresh mint sprigs, plus 2 tablespoons
　finely chopped fresh mint

In a small bowl, combine tandoori paste, 2 tablespoons yogurt, lemon zest, and lemon juice. Put chicken in a baking dish. Pour tandoori mixture over and stir until chicken is coated. Cover and refrigerate for 2 hours.

Light a fire in a charcoal grill or heat a grill pan. Brush grill or pan lightly with oil. Cook chicken for 4–5 minutes on each side, or until juices run clear when pierced with a skewer. Transfer to a cutting board and let rest for 5 minutes. Cut each tenderloin into 2 long strips (if using chicken breast fillets, slice each fillet into 4 long strips).

Using a vegetable peeler, cut carrot and cucumber into thin ribbons. To heat naan, follow instructions on packet. In a small bowl, stir ½ cup yogurt, garlic, and chopped mint together.

Place naan on a work surface. Divide chicken, cucumber, carrot, and mint leaves among naan. Drizzle with yogurt mixture. Wrap the naan around filling and serve immediately.

Makes 6 wraps

WARM TANDOORI CHICKEN WRAPS

Peking duck rolls
with chili jam

4 scallions (shallots/spring onions)

4 dinner rolls or bagels

1 tablespoon hoisin sauce

4 Chinese lettuce or butter lettuce leaves

1 carrot, peeled and cut into matchsticks
2½ inches (6 cm) long

12 oz (375 g) sliced Chinese roast duck meat
and skin

¼ cup Chili jam for serving (see page 106)

Trim scallions to 4-inch (10-cm) lengths, discarding dark green parts. Using a sharp knife, make ¼-inch (6-mm) cuts into green end of each scallion. Place in a bowl of ice water. Refrigerate until scallions curl, about 15 minutes. Drain.

Meanwhile, preheat oven to 325°F (165°C). Wrap rolls in aluminum foil, and bake for 10 minutes or until heated through. Remove from oven.

Using a serrated knife, cut each roll three-fourths open. Spread cut surface of each roll with hoisin sauce. Divide lettuce, carrot, scallion, and sliced duck among rolls. Spoon on chili jam or serve in a small bowl for dipping.

Makes 4 rolls

PEKING DUCK ROLLS WITH CHILI JAM

Wok-fried wontons

1 cup (6 oz/185 g) shredded Chinese roast duck
  meat with skin

2 scallions (shallots/spring onions), finely
  chopped

1 teaspoon peeled and grated fresh ginger

1 teaspoon grated orange zest

2 tablespoons hoisin sauce

1/2 teaspoon Asian sesame oil

16–20 square wonton skins

3 cups (24 fl oz/750 ml) vegetable or canola oil
  for deep-frying

FOR DIPPING SAUCE

2 tablespoons hoisin sauce

1 tablespoon Chinese black vinegar

1 teaspoon Asian sesame oil

In a bowl, combine duck, scallions, ginger, and orange zest. Stir in hoisin sauce and sesame oil until well combined. Place 1 wonton skin on a work surface (keep remaining skins covered with a damp cloth to prevent drying out). Place 2 teaspoonfuls of duck mixture in center. Brush edges of skin with water. Gather skin edges together and twist to seal. Repeat with remaining wonton skins and filling.

In a wok, a large, heavy skillet, or a deep fryer, heat oil to 375°F (190°C) or until a small bread cube dropped in oil sizzles and turns golden. Fry wontons in batches until golden, 1–2 minutes. Using a wire-mesh skimmer, transfer to paper towels to drain.

In a small bowl, mix all dipping sauce ingredients together. Serve wontons hot, with dipping sauce.

Makes about 16–20 wontons

Hint

You can substitute duck with roast chicken.

Roast duck and long-bean rolls

¹/₂ Chinese roast duck

1 tablespoon hoisin sauce, plus ¹/₄ cup
  (2 fl oz/60 ml) for serving

1 tablespoon orange juice

1 teaspoon soy sauce

4 scallions (shallots/spring onions), halved
  lengthwise

1 tablespoon vegetable oil

2 teaspoons peeled and grated fresh ginger

8 long beans (snake beans), cut into 3-inch
  (7.5-cm) lengths

4 pieces lavash or mountain bread

¹/₂ English (hothouse) cucumber, seeded and cut
  into 3-inch (7.5-cm) lengths

Remove meat from duck and discard bones. Slice meat and skin into strips about 3 inches (7.5 cm) long.

In a small bowl, stir 1 tablespoon hoisin sauce, orange juice, and soy sauce together. Set aside.

Place scallions in a bowl and add boiling water to cover. Let stand for 1 minute. Drain and rinse under cold running water.

Heat oil in a wok over medium heat and stir-fry ginger and long beans for 2 minutes. Add duck meat and hoisin sauce mixture. Stir-fry for 1–2 minutes, or until duck is heated through. Remove from heat and let stand for 5 minutes.

Place lavash bread on a work surface. Arrange duck stir-fry and cucumber evenly over bread. Roll each bread slice into a cylinder and tie at each end with a length of scallion. Cut each roll in half crosswise. Serve immediately.

Makes 4 rolls

ROAST DUCK AND LONG-BEAN ROLLS

pork

Vietnamese baguettes

$^1/_2$ English (hothouse) cucumber, seeded

$^1/_2$ carrot, peeled

4 scallions (shallots/spring onions)

1 long baguette (French stick)

3 oz (90 g) chicken liver pâté

8 oz (250 g) Chinese roast pork, sliced

4 thin slices ham

4 sprigs fresh cilantro (fresh coriander)

1 tablespoon light soy sauce

Using a vegetable peeler, cut carrot and cucumber into thin ribbons. Trim scallions to 4-inch (10-cm) lengths. Cut baguette crosswise into 4 equal pieces. Cut each piece in half lengthwise. Spread cut sides with pâté. Arrange pork, ham, cucumber, carrot, scallions, and cilantro in each section of baguette. Drizzle filling with soy.

Wrap each baguette in a piece of parchment (baking) paper, if desired, and serve.

Makes 4 baguettes

Tiny pork rolls

(see page 28 for step-by-step guide)

1 oz (30 g) cellophane noodles

4 oz (125 g) ground (minced) pork

2 cloves garlic, finely chopped

2 teaspoons peeled and grated fresh ginger

1 tablespoon finely chopped fresh Thai basil

1 tablespoon finely chopped fresh cilantro
  (fresh coriander)

1 bird's eye chili, seeded and finely chopped

1 teaspoon soy sauce

6 round rice paper wrappers (8 inches/20 cm)
  in diameter

1 egg, beaten

3 cups (24 fl oz/750 ml) vegetable or canola oil
  for deep-frying

Nuoc mam (Vietnamese dipping sauce)
  (see page 104)

Put noodles in a heatproof bowl and add boiling water to cover. Let soak for 10 minutes. Drain. Using scissors, coarsely cut noodles into shorter lengths. In a medium bowl, combine noodles, pork, garlic, ginger, basil, cilantro, chili, and soy sauce. Using wet hands, mix until well combined.

Using scissors, cut rice paper wrappers into quarters. Working in batches, brush each with beaten egg. Let stand for 2–3 minutes, or until softened. Place 1 heaping teaspoonful of pork mixture near rounded end of each wrapper quarter. Fold rounded end over filling, fold in sides, and roll into a small cylinder. Repeat with remaining quarters and filling.

In a large, heavy skillet, deep fryer, or wok, heat oil to 375°F (190°C) or until a small cube of bread dropped in oil sizzles and turns golden. Working with 4–6 pork rolls at a time, deep-fry until golden and crisp, 3–4 minutes. Using a wire-mesh skimmer, transfer to paper towels to drain. Serve hot, with dipping sauce.

Makes about 32 rolls

TINY PORK ROLLS

Chipolata rolls with tomato and red chili salsa

FOR TOMATO AND RED CHILI SALSA

1 large ripe tomato, finely chopped

1 bird's eye red chili, seeds removed and
  finely chopped

1 tablespoon chopped fresh Thai basil

1 tablespoon chopped fresh cilantro
  (fresh coriander)

1 clove garlic, finely chopped

3 teaspoons fresh lime juice

1 teaspoon fish sauce

1 teaspoon sesame oil

freshly ground black pepper

4 small dinner rolls

8 chipolatas (small sausages)

1 tablespoon soft butter for spreading

1 flat anchovy fillet, finely mashed

parchment (baking) paper, for serving (optional)

To make salsa: In a small bowl, combine all ingredients. Stir to blend. Set aside.

Preheat oven to 350°F (180°C). Wrap rolls in aluminum foil and bake for 10 minutes, or until just heated through.

Meanwhile, heat a grill pan over medium heat. Brush with oil and cook sausages until browned on all sides, 3–4 minutes. Remove from pan.

In a small bowl, blend butter and anchovy together. Using a serrated knife, cut each dinner roll three-fourths open. Spread cut surface of each roll lightly with anchovy butter. Place 2 warm sausages in each roll. Wrap roll with parchment paper and serve warm, with tomato and red chili salsa.

Makes 4 rolls

Pork and shrimp rolls

(see page 29 for step-by-step guide)

1 oz (30 g) cellophane noodles

4 butter lettuce leaves

4 tablespoons mayonnaise

8 round rice paper wrappers (8 inches/20 cm)
 in diameter

12 fresh mint leaves

8 oz (250 g) Chinese roast pork or barbecued pork,
 sliced

4 jumbo shrimp (king prawns), cooked, shelled,
 and deveined, then halved

Satay sauce (see page 102)

Put noodles in a bowl and add boiling water to cover. Let soak for 10 minutes. Drain. Using scissors, coarsely cut noodles into shorter lengths. Remove bottom 2 inches (5 cm) of stem from each lettuce leaf.

Fill a medium bowl with warm water. Place a kitchen towel on your work surface. For each roll, dip 2 rice paper wrappers into water for 15 seconds, or until soft. Stack wrappers on towel. Place a lettuce leaf on one side of wrapper. Top with 1 tablespoonful mayonnaise. Arrange one-eighth of noodles and pork over lettuce leaf. Top with 3 mint leaves. Starting at lettuce side of wrapper, roll halfway into a cylinder. Place 2 shrimp halves, cut-side down, on wrapper. Continue to roll into a cylinder.

Cover with a damp towel to prevent drying out. Repeat with remaining wrappers and filling. Using a sharp knife, cut each roll in half crosswise. Serve with satay sauce.

Makes 4 rolls

Spicy pork rolls

3 scallions (shallots/spring onions),
  halved lengthwise

6 oz (185 g) ground (minced) pork

2 teaspoons sambal oelek

3 cloves garlic, finely chopped

$1/4$ cup ($1/3$ oz/10 g) finely chopped fresh cilantro
  (fresh coriander)

$1/4$ teaspoon sea salt

$1/4$ teaspoon ground white pepper

1 sheet frozen puff pastry, thawed

1 egg, beaten

$1/4$ cup (2 fl oz/60 ml) light soy sauce for dipping

Put scallions in a bowl and add boiling water to cover. Let stand for 1 minute. Drain and rinse under cold running water.

Preheat oven to 450°F (230°C). Line a baking tray with parchment (baking) paper.

In a bowl, combine pork, sambal oelek, garlic, cilantro, salt, and pepper. Put puff pastry on a work surface, and cut into 4 rectangles. Place a line of pork mixture down the center of each pastry piece. Brush edges of pastries with beaten egg. Fold long ends of each pastry over pork filling, overlapping slightly and sealing to form a neat sausage roll. Trim away any excess pastry. Cut each roll into crosswise pieces 1 inch (2.5 cm) wide.

Place on prepared pan, sealed side down. Brush tops with beaten egg. Tie a scallion around each piece. Brush each again with beaten egg. Bake until golden and crisp, about 15 minutes. Remove from oven and serve hot, with soy sauce for dipping.

Makes about 12 rolls

SPICY PORK ROLLS

Thai beef salad wraps

8 fresh chives

1 oz (30 g) cellophane noodles

8 oz (250 g) beef rump steak

1 tablespoon soy sauce

2 cloves garlic, crushed

1 tablespoon shaoxing wine

4 butter lettuce leaves

$^1/_2$ English (hothouse) cucumber, seeded
   and thinly sliced

1 bird's eye chili, seeded and sliced

2 tablespoons chopped fresh cilantro
   (fresh coriander)

2 tablespoons fresh mint leaves

$^1/_2$ cup ($1^3/_4$ oz/50 g) fresh bean sprouts

$^1/_4$ cup ($1^1/_2$ oz/45 g) unsalted roasted peanuts

4 flour tortillas

FOR DRESSING

1 tablespoon fresh lime juice

1 tablespoon fish sauce

1 clove garlic, crushed

2 teaspoons shaved palm sugar or packed
   brown sugar

Put chives in a small bowl and add boiling water to cover. Let stand 30 seconds, or until softened. Drain and rinse under cold water. Set aside.

Put noodles in a bowl, and add boiling water to cover. Let soak for 10 minutes. Drain. Using scissors, coarsely cut noodles into shorter lengths.

Put rump steak in a shallow dish. In a small bowl, stir soy, garlic, and wine together. Pour over steak, cover, and refrigerate for 30 minutes. Drain. Pat steak dry with paper towels.

Heat a grill pan over medium-high heat. Brush pan with oil, add steak, and cook for 2 minutes on each side for rare. Remove from pan and let cool. Slice thinly across grain. Set aside.

Remove bottom 2 inches (5 cm) of stem from lettuce leaves. In a bowl, combine steak, noodles, cucumber, chili, cilantro, mint, bean sprouts, and peanuts.

In a small bowl, stir all dressing ingredients together until sugar dissolves. Add to salad and toss to coat evenly.

Warm flour tortillas according to instructions on packet. Place tortillas on a work surface. Place a lettuce leaf on one side of each tortilla. Spoon the salad over. Roll up and tie with 1 chive at each end of roll. Cut rolls in half crosswise to serve.

Makes 4 rolls

THAI BEEF SALAD WRAPS

Asian sausage rolls

(see page 30 for step-by-step guide)

16 Chinese pork sausages (lop chong)

4 sheets frozen puff pastry, thawed

1 egg, beaten

2 teaspoons sesame seeds

½ cup (4 fl oz/125 ml) hoisin sauce

Preheat oven to 450°F (230°C). Line a baking tray with parchment (baking) paper. Using a sharp knife, trim sausage ends. Place 1 pastry sheet on a work surface and cut into four equal pieces. Turn each square so that one corner faces you. Brush pastry edges with beaten egg. Place a sausage 1 inch (2.5 cm) from the bottom end of each pastry square. Roll bottom end of pastry over sausage. Fold in sides, then roll to form a cylinder. Brush top with beaten egg. Sprinkle with sesame seeds. Repeat with the remaining sausages and pastry.

Place rolls on prepared pan. Bake for 15 minutes, or until golden and crisp. Remove from oven. Cut each roll crosswise into 4 pieces. Serve hot, with hoisin sauce for dipping.

Makes 16 rolls

ASIAN SAUSAGE ROLLS

Melon wraps
with chili dressing

1 cantaloupe (rockmelon), halved, seeded,
 and peeled

12 very thin slices prosciutto

FOR CHILI DRESSING

$^1/_4$ cup (2 fl oz/60 ml) fresh lime juice

2 teaspoons peeled and grated fresh ginger

1 Thai red chili, seeded and sliced

1 tablespoon Asian sesame oil

$2^1/_2$ tablespoons mirin

freshly ground pepper to taste

Cut each melon half into 6 wedges. Wrap 1 slice of prosciutto around each wedge of melon. Combine all dressing ingredients in a screwtop jar and shake well to blend. Arrange melon wraps on serving plates and drizzle with dressing. Sprinkle with pepper. Serve chilled as an appetizer.

Makes 12 wraps

Prosciutto ham

A lightly salted Italian ham to wrap around fresh fruits, vegetables, or chicken breasts before baking.

MELON WRAPS WITH CHILI DRESSING

Stir-fried barbecued pork rolls

1 tablespoon plum sauce

1 tablespoon orange juice

1 teaspoon soy sauce

1 tablespoon vegetable oil

3 cloves garlic, finely chopped

1 Thai red chili, seeded and sliced

5 oz (150 g) bok choy sum, cut into $2^1/_2$-inch
  (6-cm) lengths

8 oz (250 g) Chinese barbecued pork, sliced

4 pieces mountain bread or lavash

$^1/_4$ cup fried noodles (flour sticks)

2 tablespoons fried shallots (French shallots)

$^1/_4$ cup (2 fl oz/60 ml) plum sauce, for dipping

In a small bowl, stir 1 tablespoon plum sauce, orange juice, and soy sauce together. Set aside.

Heat oil in a wok over medium heat and stir-fry garlic and chili until fragrant, about 1 minute. Add choy sum and stir-fry for 2 minutes. Add pork and plum sauce mixture. Stir-fry until pork changes color, 1–2 minutes. Remove from heat and let stand for 5 minutes.

Place bread on a work surface. Distribute pork stir-fry evenly over bread. Top with fried noodles and shallots. Roll into a cylinder and wrap in a strip of parchment (baking) paper. Cut each roll in half crosswise. Serve immediately, with plum sauce.

Makes 4 rolls

STIR-FRIED BARBECUED PORK ROLLS

Pork and betel-leaf wraps

8 oz (250 g) ground (minced) pork

3 teaspoons red curry paste

2 cloves garlic, finely chopped

1 tablespoon chopped fresh Thai basil leaves

2 tablespoons chopped fresh cilantro
(fresh coriander)

2 red bird's eye chilies, seeded and
finely chopped

1 teaspoon soy sauce

1/4 cup (1/2 oz/15 g) fresh bread crumbs

3 cups (24 fl oz/750 ml) vegetable or canola oil
for deep frying

12 fresh betel leaves

1/3 cup (3 fl oz/80 ml) Thai sweet chili sauce

In a medium bowl, combine pork, curry paste, garlic, basil, cilantro, chilies, soy sauce, and bread crumbs. Using wet hands, mix until well combined. Divide into 12 pieces and shape each into a ball.

Heat oil in a wok or large skillet over medium heat, and fry pork balls in batches until browned, 2–3 minutes. Using a wire-mesh skimmer, transfer to paper towels to drain. Let cool for 10 minutes.

Wrap each pork ball in a betel leaf and secure with a toothpick. Serve hot, with chili sauce for dipping.

Makes 12 wraps

Hint

Small butter lettuce leaves or large basil leaves can be substituted for betel leaves if not available.

Pork dumplings with chili oil

5 oz (150 g) ground (minced) pork

5 oz (150 g) jumbo shrimp (king prawns),
 shelled and deveined

2 cloves garlic, finely chopped

1 tablespoon peeled and grated fresh ginger

$1/4$ teaspoon salt

2 tablespoons chopped fresh cilantro
 (fresh coriander)

1 tablespoon chopped fresh Vietnamese mint

16 wonton skins

FOR CHILI OIL

1 tablespoon chili oil

2 teaspoons ketjap manis

1 tablespoon finely chopped garlic

1 teaspoon Chinese red vinegar

In a food processor, combine pork, shrimp, garlic, ginger, and salt. Process for 20 seconds, or until well blended. Transfer to a bowl and add cilantro and mint. Using wet hands, mix until well combined.

Place wonton skins on a work surface. Cover remaining skins with a clean damp kitchen towel. Place 1 tablespoon of pork filling in center of wonton skin and brush edges of skin with water. Gather edges around filling, forming a basket. Gently squeeze center of dumpling so that filling is exposed at top. Tap base of dumpling on work surface to flatten. Set aside on a tray and cover with plastic wrap. Repeat with remaining wonton skins and filling.

Line a medium-sized bamboo steamer with parchment (baking) paper. Fill a medium-sized wok about one-third full with water (steamer should not touch water). Bring water to a boil. Arrange dumplings in steamer. Cover with lid. Place steamer over boiling water. Steam for 12 minutes, adding more water to wok as necessary.

Meanwhile, stir all chili oil ingredients together in a small bowl. Lift steamer off wok and carefully remove dumplings from steamer. Serve hot, with chili oil for dipping.

Makes 16 dumplings

PORK DUMPLINGS WITH CHILI OIL

Vegetable spring rolls

4 dried Chinese mushrooms

1 oz (30 g) cellophane noodles

2 tablespoons vegetable or canola oil

3 cloves garlic, chopped

2 tablespoons peeled and grated fresh ginger

6 scallions (shallots/spring onions), including some
  green parts, finely chopped

2 cups (6 oz/185 g) shredded Chinese (napa) cabbage

2 medium carrots, peeled and grated

$1/3$ cup chopped fresh cilantro (fresh coriander)

1 cup ($3^1/2$ oz/105 g) fresh bean sprouts

2 tablespoons plus $1/3$ cup Thai sweet chili sauce

2 teaspoons fish sauce

18 frozen square spring roll wrappers ($8^1/2$ by
  $8^1/2$ inches/21.5 by 21.5 cm), thawed

1 egg white, lightly beaten

3 cups (24 fl oz/750 ml) vegetable or canola oil for
  deep-frying

Put mushrooms in a small bowl and add boiling water to cover. Let stand for 10 minutes. Drain, squeezing out excess liquid. Thinly slice mushrooms, discarding tough stems.

Put noodles in a bowl and add boiling water to cover. Let soak for 10 minutes. Drain. Using scissors, coarsely cut noodles into shorter lengths.

Heat oil in a wok or large skillet and stir-fry garlic and ginger for 1 minute, or until fragrant. Add scallions and cabbage. Stir-fry for 2 minutes, or until cabbage softens. Remove from heat. Stir in carrots, cilantro, bean sprouts, noodles, mushrooms, 2 tablespoons chili sauce, and fish sauce. Mix well. Let cool completely.

Place 1 spring roll wrapper on a work surface. Brush edges of wrapper with egg white. Place 1 heaping tablespoonful of filling in center of wrapper. Roll the bottom of the wrapper diagonally over filling. Fold in sides and roll up diagonally. Seal edges with egg white. Repeat with remaining wrappers and filling.

In a large wok, heat oil to 375°F (190°C), or until a small bread cube dropped in oil sizzles and turns golden. Fry spring rolls in batches until golden, about 2 minutes. Using a wire-mesh skimmer, transfer to paper towels to drain. Serve hot, with $1/3$ cup chili sauce for dipping.

Makes 18 rolls

VEGETABLE SPRING ROLLS

Asparagus and wasabi wraps

12 asparagus spears, trimmed

48 square wonton skins
  ($3\frac{1}{2}$ by $3\frac{1}{2}$ inches/9 by 9 cm)

about 1 tablespoon wasabi paste

3 cups (24 fl oz/750 ml) vegetable or canola oil
  for deep-frying

Cut each asparagus spear in half crosswise. Place 2 wonton skins on a work surface (keep remaining skins covered with a damp cloth to prevent drying out). Lightly spread 1 skin with a little wasabi paste. Place the second skin on top. Place 1 piece asparagus diagonally across one corner of stacked skins. Brush edges with water. Roll asparagus in skins, allowing one end of asparagus to protrude. Repeat with remaining skins, wasabi, and asparagus pieces.

In a large wok, heat oil to 375°F (190°C) or until a small bread cube dropped in oil sizzles and turns golden. Add wraps in batches and fry until golden, about 2 minutes. Using a wire-mesh skimmer, transfer to paper towels to drain. Serve hot.

Makes 24 wraps

Tofu and rice wraps

(see page 31 for step-by-step guide)

6 scallions (shallots/spring onions), white part
  only, finely sliced (reserve green parts)

Vinegared rice (see below)

1¹/₂ tablespoons black sesame seeds

12 fried tofu skins

¹/₃ cup (3 fl oz/80 ml) light soy sauce

VINEGARED RICE

FOR RICE

1¹/₄ cups (9 oz/280 g) short-grain rice

1¹/₄ cups (10 fl oz/300 ml) water

1¹/₂ tablespoons sake

FOR VINEGAR

1¹/₂ tablespoons sushi vinegar

¹/₄ teaspoon sea salt

1 teaspoon superfine (caster) sugar

Cut scallion greens in half lengthwise. Put in a bowl and add boiling water to cover. Let stand for 15 seconds. Drain and rinse in cold running water. Put aside.

In a bowl, combine rice, sesame seeds, and sliced scallions. Mix well. In a saucepan of boiling water, boil tofu skins for 3 minutes. Using a slotted spoon, transfer to paper towels to drain. Let cool. Cut each tofu skin in half. Open each half to make a pouch. Using wet hands, scoop up about ¼ cup rice mixture and put into a tofu pouch; do not overfill, or pouch will split. Put the filled pouches, open-side up, on a plate. Tie a green scallion length around each tofu pouch. Refrigerate for ½ hour before serving. Serve with soy sauce for dipping.

Vinegared rice: Put rice into a bowl, and add cold water to cover. Stir briskly to remove any starch. Drain. Repeat 3 times.

Pour rice and 1¼ cups water in a medium, heavy saucepan. Cover and bring to a boil. Boil for 3 minutes. Reduce heat to medium and boil for 5 minutes. Reduce heat to low and simmer until rice is tender, 5–10 minutes. Remove from heat and stir in sake. Place a kitchen towel over open pan. Replace lid and let rice stand for 15 minutes. Scrape hot rice into a shallow dish and spread out evenly. Stir rice to separate grains. Gradually stir in vinegar and continue stirring until rice is at room temperature. (Do not refrigerate.) Cover with a damp kitchen towel.

To make vinegar: In a small saucepan, combine vinegar, salt, and sugar. Stir over low heat until sugar dissolves. Remove from heat.

Makes 12

Mango and carrot fresh spring rolls

1 oz (30 g) cellophane noodles

4 iceberg lettuce leaves

8 round rice paper wrappers (8 inches/20 cm
in diameter)

1 large carrot, peeled and grated

1 mango, peeled, cut from pit, and sliced

3 oz (90 g) bean sprouts

8 fresh basil leaves

8 fresh mint leaves

Satay sauce for dipping (see page 102)

Put noodles in a bowl, and add boiling water to cover. Let soak for 10 minutes. Drain. Using scissors, coarsely cut noodles into shorter lengths. Remove the bottom 2 inches (5 cm) from each lettuce leaf stem.

Fill a bowl with warm water and place a kitchen towel on a work surface. For each roll, dip 2 rice paper wrappers in the water for 15 seconds, or until softened. Stack wrappers on towel. Arrange a lettuce leaf along one side of rice papers. Top leaf with one-fourth of noodles, carrot, mango, and bean sprouts, 2 basil leaves and 2 mint leaves. Roll into a cylinder. Cover with a damp kitchen towel to prevent drying out. Repeat with remaining wrappers and filling.

Using a sharp knife, cut each roll crosswise into 2 or 3 pieces. Serve with satay sauce.

Makes 4 rolls

MANGO AND CARROT FRESH SPRING ROLLS

Potato and mint samosas

3 large potatoes, peeled and chopped

3 oz (90 g) cooked green peas

1 teaspoon cumin seeds

2 large green jalapeno or serrano chilies, seeded
and finely chopped

1/2 red (Spanish) onion, finely chopped

3 tablespoons chopped fresh cilantro
(fresh coriander)

2 tablespoons chopped fresh mint leaves

1/3 cup (3 fl oz/80 ml) fresh lemon juice

12 sheets frozen filo pastry, thawed

1/3 cup (3 fl oz/80 ml) vegetable oil

Preheat oven to 400°F (200°C). Line a baking tray with parchment (baking) paper. In a saucepan of salted boiling water, cook potatoes until tender, about 8 minutes. Drain and mash. Let cool. In a medium bowl, combine mashed potatoes, peas, cumin seeds, chilies, onion, cilantro, mint, and lemon juice. Stir until well combined.

Place 1 sheet of filo on a work surface (keep remaining filo covered with a damp cloth). Brush filo lightly with oil. Fold in half lengthwise. Brush again with oil. Place 1 heaping tablespoonful of potato filling at one end of pastry strip. Fold corner over filling to make a triangle. Continue folding pastry in same fashion to make a neat triangular package. Place on prepared pan. Brush with oil. Repeat with remaining filo, filling, and oil. Bake for 15–20 minutes, or until golden and crisp. Serve hot.

Makes 12 samosas

POTATO AND MINT SAMOSAS

Spinach and mushroom wraps

FOR PANCAKES

$1/4$ cup (2 oz/60 g) blanched spinach

$1^1/4$ cups (10 fl oz/300 ml) milk

1 egg, beaten

$3/4$ cup (4 oz/125 g) all-purpose (plain)
  flour, sifted

$1/4$ teaspoon sea salt

olive oil for brushing

FOR FILLING

1 tablespoon olive oil

1 clove garlic, finely chopped

6 scallions (shallots/spring onions), including
  green parts, sliced

5 oz (150 g) shimeji (oyster) mushrooms,
  roughly chopped

3 oz (90 g) Swiss brown mushrooms, sliced

1 cup (7 oz/220 g) blanched spinach

2 tablespoons Thai sweet chili sauce

1 tablespoon soy sauce

1 large jalapeno or serrano red chili, seeded
  and cut into fine shreds

To make pancakes: In a food processor, process spinach until smooth, about 20 seconds. Add milk, egg, flour, and salt. Process until well blended, about 30 seconds. Transfer to a pitcher (jug).

Brush an 8-inch (20-cm) nonstick skillet with a little olive oil. Heat over medium heat. Pour a scant $1/4$ cup pancake batter into pan, swirling pan to evenly coat it with batter. Cook until lightly browned on bottom, about 1 minute. Turn pancake with a metal spatula and cook until lightly browned, about 1 minute. Transfer to a plate lined with parchment (baking) paper. Repeat with remaining batter, stacking pancakes on lined plate. Let pancakes cool to room temperature.

Meanwhile, prepare filling: Heat oil in a wok or large skillet over medium heat and sauté garlic, scallions, and mushrooms for 2–3 minutes, or until softened. Add spinach, chili sauce, and soy sauce. Stir to blend. Cook for 1 minute. Remove from heat and let cool. Transfer to a sieve and let drain briefly.

Working in batches, place pancakes on a work surface, spread with filling, and roll up. Place on serving plates and garnish with shreds of red chili.

Makes 6 wraps

Orange and chocolate spring rolls

7 tablespoons (3¹/₂ oz/105 g) unsalted butter, softened

¹/₄ cup (2 oz/60 g) superfine (caster) sugar

2 teaspoons grated orange zest

1 egg

¹/₂ teaspoon vanilla extract (essence)

³/₄ cup (3¹/₂ oz/105 g) ground almonds

3 tablespoons (1 oz/30 g) all-purpose (plain) flour

4 oz (125 g) semisweet (plain) chocolate, grated

16 frozen spring roll wrappers (8¹/₂ by 8¹/₂ inches/21.5 by 21.5 cm), thawed

1 egg white, lightly beaten

3 cups (24 fl oz/750 ml) vegetable or canola oil for deep-frying

confectioners' (icing) sugar, for dusting

In a medium bowl, beat butter, sugar, and zest together until pale and creamy, about 2 minutes. Add egg and vanilla. Mix until combined. Add ground almonds and flour, mixing until smooth. Fold in chocolate. Cover and refrigerate for 20 minutes, or until firm.

Place 1 spring roll wrapper on a work surface, with one end facing you. Brush edges with egg white. Place 1 heaping tablespoonful of chocolate filling 1 inch (2.5 cm) from end. Fold end of wrapper over filling. Fold in sides and roll into a cylinder. Seal the seam with egg white. Repeat with remaining wrappers and filling.

In a wok, heat oil to 375°F (190°C) or until a small bread cube dropped in oil sizzles and turns golden. Fry spring rolls in batches until golden, about 2 minutes. Using a wire-mesh skimmer, transfer to paper towels to drain. Serve warm, dusted with confectioners' sugar.

Makes 16 rolls

ORANGE AND CHOCOLATE SPRING ROLLS

sauces

Satay sauce

3 tablespoons smooth peanut butter

4 cloves garlic, chopped

1 teaspoon chili oil

2 tablespoons soy sauce

pinch sea salt

2 teaspoons sugar

3 tablespoons hot water

1 tablespoon hot bean paste

In a food processor, combine all ingredients and process until smooth. Store in an airtight container in the refrigerator for up to 7 days. Serve as a dipping sauce with chicken, shrimp or beef.

Makes ¾ cup (6 fl oz/180 ml)

Ginger and lime dipping sauce

1 tablespoon peeled and grated fresh ginger

$^1/_3$ cup (3 fl oz/80 ml) fresh lime juice

2 tablespoons mirin

In a screwtop jar, combine all ingredients. Shake until well combined. Serve as a dipping sauce with chicken or seafood.

Makes ½ cup (4 fl oz/125 ml)

Nuoc mam
(Vietnamese dipping sauce)

6 tablespoons (3 fl oz/90 ml) fish sauce

2 teaspoons superfine (caster) sugar

1 tablespoon rice vinegar

3 red Thai chilies, seeded and finely chopped

2 green Thai chilies, seeded and finely chopped

In a small bowl, stir all ingredients together. Cover and let stand for 1 hour. Serve as a dipping sauce for most Asian dishes.

Makes $\frac{1}{2}$ cup (4 fl oz/125 ml)

Lemon and chili dipping sauce

1 bird's eye chili, seeded and finely chopped

3 tablespoons fish sauce

$\frac{1}{4}$ cup (2 fl oz/60 ml) fresh lime juice

1 teaspoon Asian sesame oil

2 teaspoons peeled and grated fresh ginger

1 teaspoon shaved palm sugar or packed
 brown sugar

$\frac{1}{4}$ cup (2 fl oz/60 ml) fresh lemon juice

$\frac{1}{2}$ teaspoon cracked black pepper

In a small bowl, combine all ingredients and stir until sugar is dissolved. Serve as a dipping sauce with seafood, fish or chicken.

Makes $\frac{2}{3}$ cup (5 fl oz/150 ml)

NUOC MAM (VIETNAMESE DIPPING SAUCE)

Chili jam

10 dried red chili peppers

$1/3$ cup (3 fl oz/80 ml) peanut oil

1 red bell pepper (capsicum), seeded, deribbed, and chopped

cloves from 1 head garlic, coarsely chopped

6 oz (185 g) shallots (French shallots), chopped

$1/2$ cup (3 oz/90 g) shaved palm sugar or packed brown sugar

2 tablespoons tamarind paste

Put chili peppers in a bowl and add boiling water to cover. Let stand for 15 minutes, or until softened. Drain, seed and chop chilies. In a food processor, combine chilies, oil, bell pepper, garlic, and shallots. Blend until smooth, about 30 seconds.

In a wok or skillet over medium heat, cook chili mixture, stirring constantly, for 15 minutes. Add sugar and tamarind. Reduce heat to low and simmer for 10 minutes or until mixture darkens and thickens to a jam-like consistency.

Store in a sterilized jar in the refrigerator for up to 3 months. Use or serve as a spicy ingredient with chicken, pork, beef, or seafood stir-fries.

Makes $1/2$ cup (4 fl oz/125 ml)

Lime and soy dipping sauce

2 tablespoons rice vinegar

2 tablespoons light soy sauce

1 tablespoon fresh lime juice

1 scallion (shallot/spring onion), thinly sliced, including light green parts

In a small bowl, stir all ingredients together. Serve as a dipping sauce with seafood, chicken, or fish.

Makes $1/3$ cup (3 fl oz/90 ml)

CHILI JAM

Index

Guide to weights and measures

The conversions given in the recipes in this book are approximate. Whichever system you use, remember to follow it consistently, thereby ensuring that the proportions are consistent throughout a recipe.

WEIGHTS

Imperial	Metric
⅓ oz	10 g
½ oz	15 g
¾ oz	20 g
1 oz	30 g
2 oz	60 g
3 oz	90 g
4 oz (¼ lb)	125 g
5 oz (⅓ lb)	150 g
6 oz	180 g
7 oz	220 g
8 oz (½ lb)	250 g
9 oz	280 g
10 oz	300 g
11 oz	330 g
12 oz (¾ lb)	375 g
16 oz (1 lb)	500 g
2 lb	1 kg
3 lb	1.5 kg
4 lb	2 kg

VOLUME

Imperial	Metric	Cup
1 fl oz	30 ml	
2 fl oz	60 ml	¼
3 fl oz	90 ml	⅓
4 fl oz	125 ml	½
5 fl oz	150 ml	⅔
6 fl oz	180 ml	¾
8 fl oz	250 ml	1
10 fl oz	300 ml	1¼
12 fl oz	375 ml	1½
13 fl oz	400 ml	1⅔
14 fl oz	440 ml	1¾
16 fl oz	500 ml	2
24 fl oz	750 ml	3
32 fl oz	1L	4

USEFUL CONVERSIONS

¼ teaspoon	1.25 ml
½ teaspoon	2.5 ml
1 teaspoon	5 ml
1 Australian tablespoon	20 ml (4 teaspoons)
1 UK/US tablespoon	15 ml (3 teaspoons)

Butter/Shortening

1 tablespoon	½ oz	15 g
1½ tablespoons	¾ oz	20 g
2 tablespoons	1 oz	30 g
3 tablespoons	1 ½ oz	45 g

OVEN TEMPERATURE GUIDE

The Celsius (°C) and Fahrenheit (°F) temperatures in this chart apply to most electric ovens. Decrease by 25°F or 10°C for a gas oven or refer to the manufacturer's temperature guide. For temperatures below 325°F (160°C), do not decrease the given temperature.

Oven description	°C	°F	Gas Mark
Cool	110	225	¼
	130	250	½
Very slow	140	275	1
	150	300	2
Slow	170	325	3
Moderate	180	350	4
	190	375	5
Moderately Hot	200	400	6
Fairly Hot	220	425	7
Hot	230	450	8
Very Hot	240	475	9
Extremely Hot	250	500	10

First published in the United States in 2001 by Periplus Editions (HK) Ltd.,
with editorial offices at 153 Milk Street, Boston, Massachusetts 02109 and
130 Joo Seng Road, #06-01/03, Singapore 368357

© Copyright 2001 Lansdowne Publishing Pty Ltd

All rights reserved. No part of this publication may be reproduced or utilized in any form
or by any means, electronic or mechanical, including photocopying, recording, or by any information
storage and retrieval system, without prior written permission from the publisher.

Library of Congress Cataloging-in-Publication Data is available.
ISBN 0-7946-5000-7

DISTRIBUTED BY

North America, Latin America
(*English Language*)
Tuttle Publishing
364 Innovation Drive
North Clarendon, VT 05759-9436
Tel: (802) 773-8930 Fax: (802) 773-6993
Email: info@tuttlepublishing.com
www.tuttlepublishing.com

Japan
Tuttle Publishing
Yaekari Building, 3rd Floor
5-4-12 Osaki, Shinagawa-ku
Tokyo 141-0032
Tel: (03) 5437-0171 Fax: (03) 5437-0755
Email: tuttle-sales@gol.com

Asia Pacific
Berkeley Books Pte Ltd
130 Joo Seng Road #06-01/03
Singapore 368357
Tel: (65) 6280 1330 Fax: (65) 6280 6290
Email: inquiries@periplus.com.sg

Set in Frutiger on QuarkXpress
Printed in Singapore

First Edition
04 05 06 07 08 09 8 7 6 5 4 3 2